MEXICAN VEGETARIAN COOKING

D0964677

Other titles in this series

Greek Vegetarian Cooking
Indian Vegetarian Cooking
Italian Vegetarian Cooking
Oriental Vegetarian Cooking
Vegetables the French Way
Gourmet Vegetarian Feasts
Spice of Vegetarian Cooking
Traditional Vegetarian Cooking

Mexican

VEGETARIAN COOKING

EDITH METCALFE DE PLATA

Illustrated by Clive Birch

HEALING ARTS PRESS

Rochester, Vermont

Healing Arts Press
One Park Street
Rochester, Vermont 05767

Copyright © 1983, 1989 by Edith Metcalfe de Plata

All rights reserved. No part of this book may be reproduced or utilized in any form or by any means, electronic or mechanical, including photocopying, recording, or by any information storage and retrieval system, without permission in writing from the publisher.

Note to the reader: This book is intended as an informational guide. The remedies, approaches, and techniques described herein are meant to supplement, and not to be a substitute for, professional medical care or treatment. They should not be used to treat a serious ailment without prior consultation with a qualified healthcare professional.

LIBRARY OF CONGRESS CATALOGING-IN-PUBLICATION DATA

Metcalfe de Plata, Edith.
    Mexican vegetarian cooking / by Edith Metcalfe de Plata; illustrated by Clive Birch.
        p.   cm.
    ISBN 0-89281-341-5 :
    1. Vegetarian cookery. 2. Cookery, Mexican. I. Title.
TX837.M535 1989
641.5'636–dc20   89–15604
                                                                      CIP

Printed and bound in the United States

10 9 8 7 6 5

Healing Arts Press is a division of Inner Traditions International

Distributed to the book trade in Canada by Publishers Group West (PGW), Toronto, Ontario
Distributed to the health food trade in Canada by Alive Books, Toronto and Vancouver

Contents

Dedicated to those vegetarians who love Mexican foods.

Introduction

We usually think of Mexicans as consuming great quantities of meats, poultry and sea foods and although many wealthy Mexicans do feast on these products, there are millions who cannot afford them; and strangely enough, most Mexican dishes are vegetarian in practice.

There is a whole section on chilies, so there is no need to deal with them here, except to say, no Mexican dish is complete without its own particular grouping of chilies.

The recipes in this book are those used in the restaurant *Las Margarita's* on Lopez Cotilla. We had as many gringo customers as Mexican. It was amazing to discover tha thousands of Mexicans refuse to eat the meats, poultry and seafoods served in their own country and that the vegetarian restaurants operating in Mexico City and Guadalajara are as popular as their counterparts which serve meat.

Quite a few of the everyday utensils to be found in a Mexican kitchen are so different from those used in the United States that it seems important to describe some of them:

A *Chiquihuite* is used to transport hot tortillas to the dining table. It is a small, handleless basket lined with a clean napkin. The basket is the size of the usual tortilla.

A *Comal* is a clay griddle for baking and toasting.

A *Cazuela* is a casserole which is round and basin-like in form. This serves as a saucepan, frying pan, baking dish, mixing bowl and candy dish.

A *Cucharero* is a rack for wooden spoons. It is usually very decorative.

A *Machete* is a lethal weapon. It is usually about a yard long, slightly curved and very sharp. (I once saw one being used to make mincemeat of a poisonous snake!)

A *Metate* is a porous rock or grinding stone used to make the masa for tortillas, to grind chocolate, nuts, chilies and a multitude of other foods.

A *Molcajete* is a pitted, black-stone, three-legged bowl and is the Mexican version of a mortar.

A *Tejolote* is the pestle of the *molcajete*. It is cylindrical and about four inches long by two inches thick.

A *Molinillo* is a beautifully hand-carved, wooden chocolate beater which is twirled between the hands to whip the chocolate into a foam. The end of the *molinillo* is bulb-like with an unattached ring which helps to turn the liquid into a froth. Mexican chocolate is sold in small cakes which are already sugared and cinnamon-flavored.

An *Olla* is a cooking pot for soups and beans and is made of clay, as are all of the real Mexican pots.

A *Jarro* is a water pitcher which is hung to catch the least breeze which cools the water to a refrigerator temperature.

A *Soplador* is a palm leaf fan used to blow smoldering embers into a fire in a charcoal brazier.

A *Metlapil* is a cylindrical-shaped stone for grinding corn, chilies, tomatoes, nuts and other foods on a *metate*.

Typical Mealtimes in Mexico
Mexican meals never vary and, generally speaking, the same combination of foods is served every day.

6 a.m. *Merienda* – an early morning snack of chocolate or coffee with *pan dulce* (sweet rolls).

9 a.m. *Almuerzo* – a hearty breakfast.

2 p.m. *Comida* – the time that the main meal of the day is prepared and served. Seven- and eight-course dinners are not unusual.

5 p.m. *Merienda* – an afternoon snack of *antojitos* and coffee.

10 p.m. *Cena* – a supper of *café con leche* (coffee with milk) and the traditional *pan dulce* (sweet rolls).

Basic Food Values

Planning meals for a family, or even for oneself, requires some knowledge of nutrition to balance essential food requirements in a diet – especially if that is vegetarian.

The basic food elements – proteins, carbohydrates, fats, minerals and vitamins – are necessary to good health. The following sections deal with some of the functions of these essential food elements:

Proteins: Protein is required for the repair and maintenance of body tissue and for growth. Protein foods include eggs, milk, cheese, nuts and dried beans, and the amount of protein an individual needs varies according to age, body weight and rate of growth. From infancy to childhood this need is greater, per pound of body weight, than in adulthood. Pregnant and nursing women also need a large supply.

Protein can be supplied by food of plant origin, but since this substance cannot be used by the body in its original form, it is broken down into amino acids in the digestive process.

Carbohydrates: An important food source of energy, carbohydrates are more easily digested and supply energy quicker than fats or protein. This category includes the starches and sugars found in vegetables, potatoes, cereals, baked goods, jams and sweets.

Carbohydrates also provide most of the food bulk which is necessary for elimination. Carbohydrate is needed by the body for specific purposes such as to act as a source of energy for the brain.

Fats: Fats are the most concentrated source of energy, and pure oils provide about twice as many calories as proteins or carbohydrates. They supply fatty acids essential in maintaining growth and health and help make foods more palatable.

Fat deposited in tissues forms a cushioning for vital organs and serves as insulation in the retention of body heat. Fats are found in butter, margarine, salad oils, whole milk, cream and nuts.

Minerals: Minerals, in varying amounts, are necessary to life. There are more than a dozen mineral elements in the body which perform vital and specific functions. Some of the better known of these substances are sodium, calcium, iron and iodine. Sodium is found in many foods and in common table salt; this is necessary for the maintenance of a normal balance of water between cells and body fluids.

Calcium is needed to build bones and teeth, and it also aids in clotting blood. It is found in milk, milk products, and leafy green vegetables.

Iron, in combination with protein and other nutrients, forms the red blood cells that carry oxygen to the tissues. Iron is available in dried fruits, whole wheat bakery products and in leafy green vegetables. Menstruating women, pregnant women and nursing mothers require more iron than men.

Vitamins: These compounds are essential to nutrition, but they do not supply energy. The best known are vitamins A, B, C and D. Vitamin A helps prevent eye diseases; vitamin B_1 (thiamine) is necessary for the functioning of nerve tissues and stimulates the appetite; both vitamin B_2 (riboflavin) and another of the B group vitamins, niacin (nicotinic acid), are necessary for healthy skin and hair; vitamin C is needed for sound teeth and gums; vitamin D aids in the utilization of calcium and phosphorus in building bones and teeth. Vitamins are present in many foods and a balanced diet will supply all the necessary vitamins.

Foods Low in Calories
Most vegetables - except lima beans, corn. Most fruits - except avocados, bananas, persimmons, dried fruits. Eggs, buttermilk, skim milk, low-fat cottage cheese, clear vegetable soups, vegetable gelatins.

Foods High in Calories
Breads, candies, ice creams, soft drinks, peanuts and peanut butter, sauces, gravies, sugar, syrups, nuts, pies, cakes and most other desserts, milk and milk products, cream, butter, alcoholic beverages.

Foods Low in Carbohydrates
Cheese, vegetables, berries, avocados, cantaloupes, oils, milk and milk products, alcoholic beverages.

Foods High in Carbohydrates
Cakes, pies, apples, bananas, dried fruits, cookies, canned fruits, syrups, breads, breakfast cereals, flours, candies, corn, dates, figs, cranberries, ice creams, sweet potatoes, tapioca, jams, molasses, pastas.

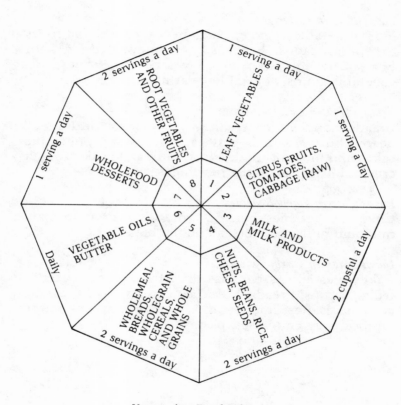

Vegetarian Food Wheel

Chilies

To name a few of the 100 known chilies in Mexico: ancho (California chili), bola, casabel, chiltepiquin, chilhuaele, chilacate, chile de arbol, chipotle, cuaresmeno, cuicateco, dulce (U.S. bell pepper), güero, jalapeño, habanero, mora, mulato, pimiento (paprika), pasilla, piquin, poblano (for chili rellenos), serrano, tornachil and xcatique.

The differences in soil, rainfall and temperatures are all deciding factors as to the size, taste and quality of a chili plant. Usually, the smaller the chili the more wallop it packs, so keep a wary eye on the jalapeños, serranos, piquins and chile de arbol (which grow on trees). The Japanese chili that has found its way into the chili factories is dried and then the outer skin is crushed and added to the seeds. Skins and seeds are mingled together to produce a very fiery spice. In Mexican homes and restaurants, the chilies used are usually bought from the markets, some fresh, others dried.

There are many ways to serve a chili: chopped, steamed, baked, powdered, stuffed, fried or pulped and maybe there are even more ways that I have forgotten or don't even know about. There is one national secret to cooking Mexico's tongue-tantalizing foods and that is never, never use only one kind of chili. Each chili has its complement, therefore it is necessary to use three or more chilies in preparing any one dish.

There are many types of chili sold either in cans or jars in many grocery stores. Different stores and supermarkets supply different brands, though, and I have tried to be general enough so that any one brand can be substituted for another.

Often when a recipe says to toast the dried chilies, it is because a toasted flavour is needed for that particular dish.

As for powdered chili, if in your area it is impossible to get the packages of chilies – ancho, mulato, pasilla, California, New Mexico (there may be others) – then by all means buy a good grade of chili powder. A rough estimate of what proportions to use when cooking with powdered chili instead of a fresh chili: 1 tablespoon of powdered chili, 1 teaspoon of whole wheat flour, 1 teaspoon of water. Personally, I hardly ever use just the prepared chili powder because there is no way of knowing what is in it – powdered twigs, leaves, branches, roots?

It should be remembered that there are differing degrees of spiciness or piquancy. Jalapeños are always hot in either the fresh or tinned form; serranos are even hotter; poblanos differ according to age but when tinned they are usually just tasty and mouth-watering; chipotles have a flavour all of their own and there is no substitute for them. Did you know that the common bell pepper is a chili and that paprika is the dried and ground product of special varieties of sweet chilies, grown in many parts of the world? I never knew until I lived in Mexico that paprika could be used in any other way except to be sprinkled, lightly, on mashed potatoes etc. But, not so. It can be used as any other chili is used; for example, Hungarians use paprika as a national flavoring.

When eating Mexican chilies, *au natural*, it is wise to have a chilled drink at your elbow. This will usually help to put out the imaginary fire slowly but efficiently.

It isn't necessary to remove the skins every time before using a chili. For some dishes the skins can be chopped with the pulp and the seeds added. For heaven's sake, don't throw away those precious seeds. They are delicious and have a decided flavor of their own. I capture every seed and use them in soups, salads, dressings, tacos, enchiladas, tamales and the whole list of Mexican and American-Mexican foods. Don't waste them – they are full of vitamins. Did you know that there are more vitamins in chilies, including the seeds, than in any other vegetable?

In the process of skinning chilies, even now, 17 years after learning the technique, I sometimes get all my fingers in the wrong places and end up with a broken and squashed pulp that has to go into a soup kettle. I find it easier, but not cheaper, to buy the *Ortega* brand of green chili (ancho or poblano), chopped or whole.

To Remove the Skins from Chilies:

Method 1: Put washed chilies into a paper bag and fasten the end with a paper clip or rubber band. Heat the oven to 400°F, put the chilies into the oven and leave them to cool for 5 minutes. Open the bag, remove the chilies, one at a time, and scrape off the skins. (Care must be used in handling the chilies so as not to split them if they are to be used for chili rellenos.)

Method 2: Place the chilies on a rack or a baking sheet. Heat the oven to 350°F and bake the chilies for 10 minutes or until the skins bubble or turn black. Remove and wrap the chilies in a damp towel or put them into a paper bag and seal it. Leave them for half an hour, then rub the skins off with a damp towel.

Method 3: Put the chilies into boiling water for 5 minutes, then dip them into cold water and rub off the skins.

Method 4: Sear the chilies over an open flame until the entire chili turns black. Place the chilies in a plastic bag and leave them for 15-20 minutes. Remove one at a time and scrape off the skin with a paring knife. (This is really the easiest method and the most widely used.)

To Make Chili Pulp:

Boil or steam the chilies for approximately 10 minutes, then split them open and scrape the softened pulp from the skin with a spoon.

Note: For further information about obtaining fresh chilies see Useful Addresses (page 125).

Coriander

In this century, coriander (cilantro) doesn't enjoy too much popularity. Coriander plants are seed annuals that grow in abundance in the Near East, Argentina, France, Morocco and Rumania. The Egyptian tombs of the twenty-first dynasty contained coriander seeds which had been entombed with the bodies for use on their further travels. The Chinese, in ancient days, believed that the consumption of coriander seeds would guarantee immortality.

Today we eat coriander because its flavor is distinctive and delicious. When ripe coriander seeds are ground to a powder they have a sweet pungency which is ideal for mixing with other herbs, spices and chilies. Curry has to have ground coriander seeds for its manufacture and the powder is also used in making breads and pickling. Try adding a couple of crushed coriander seeds to a cup of hot, black coffee. Let it brew for a couple of minutes and then sip slowly. It is very exotic.

Coriander is used as a fresh herb in Mexico and some European countries for flavoring tacos, enchiladas, empanadas, salads and sauces. Fresh coriander is usually referred to as "cilantro". Chop two to three sprigs of fresh leaves and sprinkle them over the top of a prepared dish. At first glance, fresh coriander resembles the parsley or watercress with which it is usually displayed in grocery stores. I have to pinch off a leaf and identify it by its strong and different scent. As a fresh herb the taste is quite often an acquired one but once the liking for it is established, it is considered indispensable.

Tomatillos

A Mexican kitchen can't operate without the ever-abundant tomatillo. Tomatillos have the appearance of a small green tomato, but there the similarity ends, since they have a quite distinctive taste and are handled as a separate vegetable.

I teach Mexican cooking in the San Dieguito Adult School System in California and one of my students once brought me so many tomatillos that I had to learn different ways of using them. The following ideas are ones which I worked out for myself and now use in my school-teaching.

The easiest tomatillos to handle are those that are about the size of a golf ball or larger. When ripe, the paper-like husk will have separated from the tomatillo and turned a tan colour, but it will be attached to the vegetable at the stem end. Pull the husk back over the stem end and twist to separate the husk and stem from the tomatillo. Wash in clear, cool water to cleanse off the sticky substance.

Tomatillos will stay firm and usable for months if stored with their husks on in a cool, dry area. This vegetable originated in Mexico and has, gradually, worked its way into the U.S. markets. So many people from the U.S. have lived in Mexico for some time and have become acquainted with this vegetable that it is about time there were recipes available on how to use them.

Tomatillos never have to be skinned, and cooking before using them is unnecessary; just chop, dice or blend them. They have a tart flavor but are never offensive or sharp.

Note: If tomatillos are not available, green tomatoes may be used instead.

Tomatillos in Salads
Remove the husks and stems and wash the tomatillos. Dice them in approximately half-inch squares and add them to any salad. They are delicious in fruit salads but slice them very thinly for this purpose. Add approximately ½ cup of diced tomatillos to a large bowlful of salad until you find a mixture that suits you. (It is not necessary to include red tomatoes when using tomatillos.)

Tomatillos in Soups
Remove the husks and stems and wash the tomatillos, then quarter and blend them in a blender. Add the liquid to soups in a 1-4 ratio. In a vegetable soup or stew the tomatillos can be used either diced or blended.

Tomatillos in Drinks
Remove the husks and wash the tomatillos. Quarter and blend them. Add 1 cup of liquid tomatillos to 3¼ cups of tomato juice. If making a fresh vegetable drink, add 1 tomatillo to any grouping of fruits or vegetables. A glass

of tomatillo juice by itself is delicious; just add a pinch of sea salt.

Freezing Tomatillos
Remove the husks and stems and wash the tomatillos. Quarter and blend them. Put the liquid in freezer bottles and freeze. (I use *Schweppes* club soda bottles – small size.) Leave about 1 inch of free space at the top so that the bottles won't break.

Tomatillos with Fried Potatoes
Remove the husks and stems and wash the tomatillos. Dice them and add them to some fried potatoes. Season as usual and add some grated cheese when the potatoes are almost ready to serve. Allow the cheese to melt through the potatoes.

Tomatillos in Casseroles
Remove the husks and stems and wash the tomatillos. Dice or blend them and add them to liquids to be used in casseroles. Use ¼ cup to 1 quart of casserole. Add a few jalapeño seeds for a particularly tasty effect.

Tomatillo Jam
Remove the husks and stems and wash 4 pounds of tomatillos. Quarter and blend them. (This should make 2 quarts of liquid.) Add 6 cups of raw cane sugar, 1 teaspoon of aniseed and ¼ teaspoon ground cloves. Bring the mixture to the boil slowly, stirring frequently until the sugar dissolves. Simmer, uncovered, for 1 hour or until the mixture is of jam consistency. Stir often enough so that the jam doesn't stick to the bottom of the pan and burn. (Use at least a 5-quart pan for this.)

Tomatillo Sauce
Remove the husks and stems and wash the tomatillos. Quarter and blend them. To 2 cups tomatillo liquid, add ½ cup of raw cane sugar, 1 teaspoon of celery seed, ¼ teaspoon of sea salt, ¼ teaspoon of allspice, pinch of

garlic powder and ¼ teaspoon of onion powder. Use this sauce with textured vegetable protein "meat" dishes. Sometimes it takes more than 30 minutes for the sauce to thicken.

Jicama (Pronounced HE-CA-MA)

1. Usually served cold, in round slices, covered with lemon juice and chili powder.

2. Dice and serve in salads.

3. Fry as potatoes, steam or boil. Serve hot with butter, sea salt and chili powder.

4. Cut into squares and serve on cocktail sticks with a dipping sauce, as hors d'oeuvre.

Note: Water chestnuts may be used instead of jicama where these are not available.

Garnishes for Mexican Dishes
Fruits: Cherries, oranges, grapefruits, lemons, strawberries, pears, grapes, mangos, papaya, apples, pineapple, avocado, bananas.

Vegetables: Lettuces, bean sprouts, tomatoes, mushrooms, parsley, coriander (cilantro), cucumber, radishes, scallions, white onions, zucchini, carrots, lentils, peas, garlic, chives, spinach, celery, cabbage, chilies and chili seeds.

Dairy Products: Cottage cheese, cream cheese, sour cream and many others.

Miscellaneous: Raisins, nuts, ginger, horseradish, orange and lemon peel, coconut, olives, pimento, capers, onions, mint leaves, and many others.

1. How to Make Tortillas

Early morning in Mexico finds millions of hands pat-pat-patting freshly made *masa* into tortillas. Without tortillas there would be no huevos rancheros, tacos, enchiladas, entojitos, tortas sopes, nachos or quesadillas. The tortilla is the national bread of all Mexicans, and it is made from corn.

Among the country people, knives, forks and spoons are almost unknown – the tortilla is the only eating utensil. Even soup can be eaten with a tortilla – although it is an art that has to be acquired. Eating this way, of course, cannot be done in the upright position we are familiar with. To use a tortilla as a spoon for soup one needs to almost put one's face into the soup and then scoop it up rapidly. As a newcomer to this art I had to learn how to bend my backbone at the dinner table and to talk between scoops with my eyes peering up at a new angle.

Tortillas are unleavened, thin, flat, crepe-like bread. Making them from scratch the Mexican way can be a complicated job, but there are easier ways. It is possible to buy *masa harina* from specialty food shops. *Masa harina* is a specially prepared corn flour to which all you have to do is add water to make the dough for your tortillas. Easiest of all is to buy ready-made tortillas, but it is more satisfying to make your own, and you have control over the ingredients.

You don't even have to use *masa harina*. It is possible to make tortillas by using a mixture of medium cornmeal and whole wheat flour, or even just whole wheat flour. They are not quite the authentic thing, but the ingredients may come more readily to hand.

However, for interest's sake I will go through the process of making tortillas the Mexican way. The first step is to soak overnight 2 pounds corn kernels in water to which 2 ounces slaked lime has been added. In the morning the soaked grain is boiled until the skins on the kernels begin to loosen. It is then allowed to cool to a point where the hands can be comfortably immersed in the water to rub the skins off the kernels. Once this is done the skinned grain is washed in cold water. The result is called *nixtamal*, and this is then pounded into the tortilla dough known as *masa*. The dough is kneaded and divided up into balls which are patted out into flat circular tortillas ready for the pan. It sounds easy, but as with most things there is an art to it which has to be learned.

If you start with *masa harina*, though, the whole thing becomes very much easier, and you will find instructions on the packet. Failing this, here's a recipe to try:

1 cup whole wheat flour
1 cup medium cornmeal
5 tablespoons polyunsaturated margarine
½ teaspoon sea salt
Enough water to form soft ball

1. Mix the flour and cornmeal together and blend in the margarine.

2. Add enough water to form a soft ball.

3. Knead the dough and pinch off walnut-sized pieces, rolling them into balls. Using a rolling pin, roll these out into thin circles about 5 inches in diameter.

4. Place each circle of dough into an ungreased frying pan over a high heat and allow it to cook until the dough bubbles, then turn it over and wait for the bubbles again (it takes about a minute on each side).

5. Once cooked, put your tortillas one on top of another in a basket lined with several thicknesses of napkin or towel. Lift the napkin each time you add a tortilla and close it again quickly to keep them warm. They are now ready to eat and are best hot.

As a reward for making your first tortillas, try the following titbit. It's called Chicano Pizza.

1. Fry a tortilla in deep vegetable fat until golden brown, then drain it well but keep it hot.

2. Spread grated cheese on the top and broil until the cheese is bubbly.

3. Remove the pizza and sprinkle with sea salt. Eat once once.

This can be topped with a variety of chopped chilies.

2. Soups and Starters

SPAGHETTI SOUP
Sopa de Pasta

(Serves 4)

8 ounces thin spaghetti, cooked and drained
A little vegetable oil
2 tomatoes, chopped
½ jalapeño chili, chopped
½ cup each of chopped onion and tomato sauce
¼ cup refried beans
¼ teaspoon each of sea salt, freshly ground black
    pepper, mustard, tarragon, celery seed and chopped
    parsley
Parsley, grated cheese and slivered radishes

1. Sauté the spaghetti in the oil until crisp, then drain off
   the oil. Add the tomatoes, chili, onion, tomato sauce,
   beans and seasonings and simmer for 15 minutes.

2. Serve in heated ceramic bowls and garnish with parsley,
   cheese and radishes.

PEANUT SOUP
Sopa de Cacahuate

(Serves 2)

1 tablespoon butter
1 tablespoon whole wheat flour
¼ cup chopped onion
¼ teaspoon each of sea salt, freshly ground black
    pepper, mace, chopped parsley, basil and grated
    lemon rind
2 cups milk
¼ cup peanut butter
Slivered almonds

1. Melt the butter, mix in the flour and add the onion and
    seasonings.

2. Simmer for a few minutes over low heat, then add the
    milk and peanut butter.

3. Serve the soup hot in heated soup bowls and garnish
    with the almonds.

BLACK BEAN SOUP
Sopa de Frijoles Negros

(Serves 8-10)

2 cups black beans
2½ quarts water
½ cup vegetable oil
2 cloves garlic, minced
2 onions, chopped
½ teaspoon each of sea salt, freshly ground black
   pepper, fennel seed and basil
1 teaspoon each of raw cane sugar, mustard, grated
   lemon rind and celery seed
¼ teaspoon allspice
3 tablespoons pure lemon juice
1 cup tomato sauce
Sour cream and grated cheese

1. Combine the beans and water and bring to the boil for
   10 minutes, then cover the pan, remove it from the
   heat and set it aside for 1 hour.

2. Add the oil, garlic, onions and seasonings. Cover the
   pan again and simmer the soup for 2-3 hours or until
   the beans are soft.

3. Add the lemon juice and tomato sauce. Remove a few
   tablespoons of beans and whirl them in a blender, then
   return them to the pan.

4. Reheat the soup and serve with the sour cream and
   grated cheese on top.

Antojitos are small bite-sized titbits, much the same as our canapés or *hors d'oeuvre*. The following is one of the less exotic but tasty antojitos.

NACHOS

Deep-fry some, one at a time, until golden brown and crispy. Lay them out on a baking sheet and cover them with grated, sharp cheese. Sprinkle with jalapeño seeds and broil them until the cheese is bubbly. Sprinkle a little sea salt over the top if desired and serve hot.

Note: Some nachos are served with sour cream, guacamole and salsa picante, either spread on the grilled nachos or served in separate bowls.

SAUTÉED JALAPEÑOS

Fried jalapeños are very hot; however they are also quite delicious when served in warmed or fried tortillas.

1 fresh jalapeño per serving
A little vegetable oil
1 tortilla per serving

1. Wash the jalapeños, but leave the stems in place.

2. Fry them in vegetable oil until very dark brown all over, then fold each one in a warmed tortilla, as if into an envelope.

Note: These can be served as they are or fried in vegetable oil until the tortillas are a golden brown. Sprinkle lightly with sea salt, and serve them hot.

AVOCADO DIP
Guacamole

1 medium-sized avocado, peeled and mashed
1 tomatillo or green tomato, chopped
¼ cup chopped onion
1 serrano chili, finely chopped, or 1 tablespoon salsa
 picante
2 tablespoons vegetable oil
1 tablespoon chopped cilantro
1 teaspoon chili powder
1 teaspoon cider vinegar

1. Combine all the ingredients and mix them well using
 wooden or ceramic utensils because metal tends to
 turn avocados an unhealthy-looking black. (The
 avocados are perhaps best mixed in at the last minute.)
 Serve with tortilla chips.

Note: Guacamole can be frozen, believe it or not, as long
as care is taken. It must be packed into a small-necked
container, leaving no air space. Pour vegetable oil, to the
depth of ¼ inch, on top of the guacamole; this seals out
the air which would turn the avocados black. When
thawing, leave the cover on the jar and when thoroughly
thawed, mix the oil into the avocado.

BEAN DIP
Frijoles Antojitos

1-pound can pinto beans
3 ounces cream cheese
1 tablespoon tarragon vinegar
¼ teaspoon each of garlic and onion powders, celery
    seed, curry powder and oregano
1 teaspoon each of chopped cilantro and jalapeño chili
1 tomato or 3 tomatillos, chopped
½ cup chopped onions
1 cup sour cream
¼ cup each of chopped pimento and celery
Enough tomato sauce to make a dipping consistency

1. Mash together the beans and their juice, cream cheese,
   vinegar and seasonings.

2. Mix in the rest of the ingredients and refrigerate the dip
   before serving.

3. Serve with tortilla chips.

STUFFED MUSHROOMS
Champinones Rellenos

1 pound mushrooms
1 cup cottage cheese
¼ cup each of mayonnaise, chopped peanuts, pimento,
   tomatillos, onion and carrots
¼ teaspoon each of sea salt, chopped parsley, grated
   orange rind, aniseed and seeds of hot chilies
Chopped almonds, toasted sesame seeds and shredded
   cabbage

1. Cut out the mushroom stalks as far as possible without
   cutting into dome.

2. Soak the domes in salted water for 30 minutes, then
   chop the stalks and add them to the cottage cheese and
   remaining ingredients (except the almonds, seeds and
   cabbage).

3. Stuff the filling into the domes and dip them in the
   almonds or sesame seeds. Refrigerate and serve the
   mushrooms on trays of shredded cabbage.

CHEESE SANDWICHES
Quesadillas

These are a rare treat when made according to tradition, but like everything else, shorter methods are quicker and less troublesome. I'll give both ways, the authentic and the gringo version.

1. When fresh tortillas are placed on a grill they will separate and one layer will puff-up like a half-balloon. When this happens, split the tortilla with a sharp knife along the seam side enough to open it so as to be able to insert a piece of cheese.

   Insert the cheese and immediately close the flap well so that the cheese won't run out when it melts.

   Flip the tortilla back and forth until the cheese is melted and the tortilla is golden brown and crispy. The quesadilla should be flipped only twice but until one knows what one is doing, just flip it as many times as are necessary to get a nice brown on both sides. Sprinkle with a mild sea salt.

2. The other method is to lay a tortilla flat and place a slice of cheese on the lower half. Sprinkle with jalapeño seeds and close the upper half of the tortilla over the cheese.

   Heat ¼ cup vegetable oil in a frying pan. Lay the tortilla in the oil and press it down with the back of a spatula so that all areas of the tortilla will be crisp. Do the same on the other side and then drain the tortilla on a paper towel. Sprinkle with mild sea salta on one side only while still hot.

Note: A must in almost all Mexican cheese dishes is the need to use pure cheese and not one of the processed cheeses. A processed cheese either runs in all directions or won't spread at all.

MELTED CHEESE
Queso Fondido

Queso fondido is another delicious cheese dish of Mexico.
The equivalent of 2 slices of real (not processed) cheese is
placed in a flat earthenware dish the size of a saucer and
then melted in a hot oven.

Heat the tortillas on a griddle and place them in a
folded napkin in a basket. Keep them as hot as possible
and place the melted cheese and the hot tortillas on the
table at the same moment.

The next step requires speed and skill!

If four people are going to partake, run a sharp knife over
the cheese dividing it into four sections. As you will see,
the cheese begins immediately to reclaim its wholeness,
but the markings should guarantee that each eater has a
boundary to stay within!

Each person takes a hot tortilla and, using a blunt knife,
scrapes up one portion of the hot cheese onto the tortilla
– then roll it up and it is ready to eat. If you have time,
lightly salt the outside with a mild sea salt.

Note: One saucer of cheese serves only four people and
one queso fondido is never enough. Allow at least three
per person and have the melted cheese emerging from
the stove as it is needed – never before.

PUMPKIN SEEDS
Roasted Pepitas

1⅓ cups water
3 tablespoons sea salt
1⅔ cups hulled pumpkin seeds

1. Bring the water and salt to the boil and stir until the salt is dissolved.

2. Pour the water over the seeds in a bowl, then cover them and leave them to stand for 12-24 hours.

3. Drain the water from the seeds, spread them evenly on a baking sheet and bake at 350°F for 25-35 minutes or until the seeds are dry and puffy and the kernels are separated in the center.

4. Stir the seeds frequently, leave them to cool and stir them occasionally again. Store in an air-tight container.

Note: Pepitas are usually served with antojitos.

1. BROILED CHEESE SANDWICH
Cazuela de Queso Asado

Arrange 2 slices of whole wheat bread in a buttered casserole. Spread the slices with butter and chopped green chili. Sprinkle with ¾ cup of grated cheese, a little garlic powder and toasted sesame seeds. Broil until the cheese is golden brown and bubbly. To serve, sprinkle with paprika and garnish with parsley and lemon wedges or orange slices and jalapeño.

2. BROILED CHEESE SANDWICH WITH TOMATO AND ONIONS
Cazuela de Queso con Jitomates y Cebolla Asada

Cover the basic cheese sandwich with tomato or tomatillo slices, ¼ cup of chopped onions and 2 tablespoons of chopped black olives.

3. BROILED CHEESE SANDWICH WITH MUSHROOMS AND OLIVES
Cazuela de Queso con Champinones y Aceitunas Asado

Cover the basic cheese sandwich with ½ cup of sliced mushrooms, ¼ cup of chopped black olives and 2 table-spoons of chopped onions.

4. BROILED CHEESE SANDWICH WITH ZUCCHINI AND SUNFLOWER SEEDS
Cazuela de Queso con Calabacitos y Semillas de Girasol Asada

Cover the basic cheese sandwich with ¾ cup of finely sliced zucchini, ¼ cup of sunflower seeds and 2 tablespoons of capers.

5. BROILED CHEESE SANDWICH WITH BEANS AND CHILIES
Cazuela de Queso con Frijoles y Chilis Asada

Cover the basic cheese sandwich with ½ cupful of refried beans (page 71), ¼ cup of chopped pimento and 2 tablespoons of chopped onions. Sprinkle with jalapeño seeds.

BROILED SAUERKRAUT SANDWICH
Cazuela de Col Agria Asada

(Makes 10 casseroles)

2 slices rye bread per casserole (20 slices)
Butter and mustard to spread on bread
5 cups sauerkraut, drained
½ teaspoon caraway seeds
½ cup each chopped onion and apple sauce
2½ cups grated cheese
2½ cups sour cream
Paprika, orange slices, lemon wedges, chili seeds

1. Lay 2 slices of bread in the base of each buttered sandwich casserole and spread with butter and mustard.

2. Combine the sauerkraut, caraway seeds, onion and apple sauce and cover the bread with ½ cupful of sauerkraut filling and ¼ cup of cheese. Broil until the cheese is bubbly.

3. To serve, cover each casserole with 4 tablespoons of sour cream, sprinkle with paprika and garnish with orange slices and/or lemon wedges and chili seeds. Serve hot and bubbly.

Note: Any part of the filling can be frozen if it isn't used the first time.

EMPANADAS
Pastelillos de Queso

(Makes 4 dozen)

2 cups *masa harina**
½ teaspoon each of sea salt and baking powder
¼ cup butter
1 egg, beaten
½ cup water
1 tablespoon chopped jalapeño chilies
4 cups grated sharp cheese
Sesame seeds and salsa picante (page 60)

1. Sift the flour, salt and baking powder into a bowl.

2. Rub in the butter (as for making a pie crust) and mix in the egg, water and jalapeño chili.

3. Roll the dough into a ball, wrap it in wax paper and refrigerate it for 1 hour.

4. Divide the dough into thirds. Roll each third out on a floured surface until the dough is ⅛ inch thick, then cut it into 2½-3-inch circles and moisten the edges with water.

5. Place 1 teaspoon of cheese in each circle, fold the circle in half and press the edges down with a fork to seal them.

6. Fry the empanadas in deep vegetable oil at 350°F for a few minutes or until golden brown.

Note: As the empanadas rise to the surface, spoon a little oil over the tops to make them puff up. Turn them over to brown and drain them on paper towels. Serve hot or cold with a sauce to dip them into.

*Available at specialty food stores. See Useful Addresses (page 125).

3. Salads and Salad Dressings

Salad Greens
Leave these whole, tear them or shred them; use them in various combinations or serve them separately:
Various types of lettuce, kale, spinach, endive, Swiss chard, chicory, Chinese cabbage, and parsley.

Salad Ingredients
Each of these foods may be used with other fruits or vegetables: Tomatoes, cucumber, zucchini, carrots, bean sprouts, avocado, brussels sprouts, cottage cheese, cabbage, peas, beets, green beans, lima beans, snap beans, red kidney beans, fruit, mushrooms, chick-peas (garbanzo beans) and jicama.

Salad Garnishes
Each of these ingredients can be used in larger or smaller quantities: Onion, green pepper, sweet red pepper, olives, cheese, lemon rind, celery, pimento, raisins, nuts, coconut, capers, green onions (scallions), shallots, radishes, garlic, chestnuts, jalapeños, parsley and chives.

Salad Seeds
These seeds can be added to the dressing or sprinkled on the salad before serving:
Dill, sesame, caraway, cardamom, cumin, sunflower, chili and celery.

AVOCADO SALAD WITH COTTAGE CHEESE AND CANDIED GINGER
Ensalada de Aguacate con Queso de la Casita

(Serves 4)

Make a bed of lettuce on each place. Place scoops of cottage cheese on the lettuce and decorate the cheese with slices of avocado, a little candied ginger and slivered almonds. Serve with Avocado Dressing (page 53).

LENTIL SALAD
Ensalada de Lentejas

(Serves 4-6)

3 cups lentils, cooked, seasoned and drained
2 tablespoons each of chopped onions and Ortega chilies
¼ cup each of chopped tomato and pimento
4 tablespoons cider vinegar
½ cup each of mayonnaise and peas
¼ teaspoon each of celery seed, sesame seed, sea salt, red pepper flakes, garlic powder, marjoram and basil
Lettuce, tomato slices and cheese wedges

1. Combine all the ingredients, except for the lettuce.

2. Make a bed of lettuce on each plate and divide the lentil mixture among them.

3. Arrange the tomato slices and cheese wedges around the dishes.

MOLDED CARROT SALAD
Ensalada de Zanahorias I

(Serves 8)

1 cup cold water
2 tablespoons unflavored gelatin
1 cup each of sour cream, carrot juice, orange juice and
   cottage cheese
2 cups grated raw carrots
½ cup each of crushed pineapple, raisins and chopped
   nuts
¼ teaspoon each of sea salt, celery seed, paprika and
   horseradish
¼ cup chopped Ortega chilies
Lettuce leaves and maraschino cherries, chopped

1. Soak the gelatin in cold water for 5 minutes. Heat over low heat to dissolve.

2. Mix in the sour cream, juices, cottage cheese, carrots, pineapple, raisins, nuts, seasonings and chilies.

3. Divide the mixture among eight individual casseroles or one large one and refrigerate for 6-8 hours. Turn the mold out onto lettuce leaves or nests and decorate with the cherries. Serve with any of the salad dressings (page 52-58).

BEAN SPROUT SALAD
Ensalada de Germain de Frijoles

(Serves 4-6)

1 pound bean sprouts (any kind)
4 tablespoons tarragon vinegar
3 tablespoons each of raw cane sugar, soy sauce and
  sesame oil
1½ teaspoons each of mustard, sea salt, freshly ground
  black pepper and paprika
½ cup chopped nuts
1 tablespoon aniseed

1. Combine all the ingredients except for the nuts and
   aniseed.

2. Marinate the sprouts for 12-24 hours, drain them and
   serve with the nuts and aniseed.

STUFFED TOMATO "FLOWERS"
'Flores' de Jitomates Rellenos

(Serves 4-6)

6 medium-sized or 4 large tomatoes
6 lettuce leaves
½ cupful sour cream
¼ cupful each of grated zucchini, chopped almonds,
    grated carrots, sliced cucumber, raisins, chopped
    Ortega chili, celery and onion
½ teaspoon each of sea salt, aniseed, dill seed, parsley,
    thyme, mace and chili powder
1 small jar sliced pimento

1. Wash and cut out the centres of the tomatoes. Slice
   downward – almost to the bottom – so the tomatoes
   will open yet remain held together at the bottom. Make
   4-6 cuts and lay the tomatoes on a bed of lettuce leaves.

2. Make a filling with the remaining ingredients (except
   for the pimento) and use it to stuff the tomatoes.

3. Garnish with pimento strips and refrigerate the salad
   until time to serve.

TOSSED GREEN SALAD
Ensalada Verde

(Serves 4-6)

1 small turnip, grated
1 cupful each of finely sliced cauliflower, zucchini and
     mushrooms
½ cup finely sliced cucumber, onion and celery, chopped
¼ cup chopped pimento
8-10 olives, quartered
3 hard-boiled eggs, halved, quartered, or sliced
½ cup each of sour cream or natural yogurt and
     mayonnaise
1 teaspoon cider vinegar
½ teaspoon each of chili powder, paprika, sea salt,
     garlic powder, celery seed, cilantro and red hot chili
     seeds

1. Combine all the ingredients except the cream, mayonnaise, vinegar and seasonings. Refrigerate the salad
until ready to serve.

2. Blend the remaining ingredients and pour the dressing
over the salad.

RAW CARROT SALAD
Ensalada de Zanahorias II

(Serves 6-8)

4 cups grated carrots
1 red apple, chopped
1 cup pineapple chunks
2 tablespoons each of lemon juice and grated orange
    rind
½ cup each of sunflower seeds and sour cream
¼ teaspoon each of sea salt, celery seeds, garlic powder,
    onion powder, dill seeds and chili powder
¼ cup chopped Ortega chilies
1 teaspoon cider vinegar

1. Mix all the ingredients together gently and refrigerate.

2. Serve on a bed of lettuce leaves.

MELON BOAT SALAD
Ensalada de Mélon

(Serves 2)

Cut a chilled melon in half, clean out the seeds and membrane, and lay it on a bed of salad greens. Fill each cavity with ½ cup of cottage cheese and decorate the cheese with chopped nuts and maraschino cherries. Use a fruit salad dressing for the finishing touch.

THREE BEAN SALAD
Ensalada de Tres Frijoles

(Serves 8)

Mix 2 cups snap beans, ½ cup onions and ¼ cup chopped pimento

Mix 1 cup cooked red kidney beans and ½ cup chopped celery

Mix 1 cup lima beans and ½ cup sliced black olives

Mix and divide among the 3 bean dishes:

    ¾ cup vegetable oil

    ¼ cup tarragon vinegar

    ½ teaspoon chopped jalapeño chili

    1 teaspoon each of sea salt, red pepper flakes, celery seed, grated lemon rind, mustard, garlic powder, onion powder, raw cane sugar and dill seeds

1. Place a bed of lettuce in the center of a large serving dish and place the snap-bean mixture on the leaves.

2. Make smaller nests of red kidney beans and lima beans around the snap beans. Refrigerate the salad and serve with lemon wedges.

ORANGE SALAD I
Ensalada de dos Tipos de Naranjas

(Serves 4-6)

1 head of lettuce
2 cups cottage cheese
4 maraschino cherries, chopped
4 oranges, peeled and sliced
4 tangerines, peeled and sectioned
2 cups shredded coconut
½ cup walnuts or other chopped nuts

1. Make a bed of lettuce leaves on a large serving plate and pile the cottage cheese in the middle of the lettuce. Sprinkle with chopped cherries.

2. Place the orange slices, overlapping each other, around the outer edge of the serving plate.

3. Lay the tangerine sections over the top of the cottage cheese and pile the coconut between the two types of oranges, like a crown.

4. Sprinkle the chopped nuts over the coconut and serve with a fruit salad dressing.

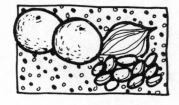

ORANGE SALAD II
Ensalada de Naranja

(Serves 6)

For Salad:
1 head of lettuce, shredded
2 oranges, peeled and thickly sliced
1 cucumber, unpeeled and thinly sliced
1 onion, cut into rings
1 chili poblano or green pepper, cut into rings

For Dressing:
3 tablespoons sesame oil
1 tablespoon wine vinegar
¼ teaspoon each of sea salt, chopped cilantro, freshly
  ground black pepper and cumin seeds
1 tablespoon chopped parsley

1. Arrange the salad ingredients in a salad bowl.

2. Put all dressing ingredients into a bottle and shake
   them well. Pour the dressing over the salad just before
   serving.

LAS MARGARITAS DRESSING
Aderezo de las Margaritas

½ cup mayonnaise
¼ cup each of orange juice, coconut (milk or ground),
    raisins, chopped maraschino cherries and chopped
    nuts
¼ teaspoon each of sea salt, ginger, aniseed, grated
    orange rind and tarragon vinegar
2 cups heavy cream

1. Combine all the ingredients with a wire whisk.

2. Refrigerate.

AVOCADO DRESSING
Aderezo de Aguacate

2 cups mayonnaise
1 cup sour cream
¼ cup Ortega chilies
2 tablespoons orange juice
2 avocados, peeled and pitted
¼ teaspoon each of sea salt, freshly ground black
    pepper, allspice and dill seeds
1 tablespoon grated orange rind

1. Combine all the ingredients, except for the orange
   rind, in a blender and blend for 1 minute.

2. Add the orange rind and refrigerate the dressing.

FRUIT SALAD DRESSING
Aderezo de Frutas

2 cups mayonnaise
1 cup cream
¼ cup each orange juice, banana and apple sauce
¼ teaspoon each of aniseed, ginger and nutmeg
½ cup each of maraschino cherries, chopped, and
  strawberries, quartered

1. Combine all the ingredients, except for the cherries
   and strawberries, in a blender and mix for 1 minute.

2. Mix in the cherries and strawberries by hand and
   refrigerate.

GARLIC DRESSING
Aderezo de Ajo

2 cups mayonnaise
1 cup sour cream
¼ cup each of lemon juice and chopped onion
4 cloves garlic
1 teaspoon cider vinegar
¼ teaspoon each of sea salt, red pepper flakes, celery
  seed, mustard and horseradish

1. Combine all the ingredients in a blender, mix for 1
   minute.

2. Refrigerate.

ONION DRESSING
Aderezo de Cebolla

2 cups mayonnaise
1 cup sour cream
2 tablespoons cider vinegar
¾ cup chopped onion
¼ teaspoon each of sea salt, freshly ground black pepper, dill seed, horseradish, oregano, thyme, rosemary and chili powder
1 tablespoon chopped parsley

1. Combine all the ingredients, except the parsley, in a •blender and mix for 2 minutes.

2. Mix in the parsley by hand and refrigerate.

PIQUANT FRENCH DRESSING
Aderezo Picante de Francesca

1 cup tarragon vinegar
2 cups peanut oil
¼ cup each of raw cane sugar, chopped onions, tomatoes
   and almonds
¼ teaspoon each of sea salt, red pepper, horseradish,
   oregano, thyme and celery seed
1-2 jalapeño chilies
2 cloves garlic
1 tablespoon each of chopped parsley, serrano chilies,
   black olives and mushrooms

1. Combine all the ingredients, except the parsley, serranos, black olives and mushrooms, in a blender and mix for 1 minute.

2. Mix in the remaining ingredients by hand, then refrigerate the dressing.

CURRY DRESSING
Aderezo de Curri

1 cup sour cream
½ cup mayonnaise
1 tablespoon each of lemon juice and grated orange
   rind
2½ tablespoons each of curry powder and dried coconut
¼ teaspoon each of sea salt, ginger, mace and aniseed
¼ cup chopped nuts

1. Combine all the ingredients, except the nuts, in a
   blender and mix for 1 minute.

2. Mix in the nuts by hand and refrigerate the dressing.

4. Sauces and Relishes

Serrano Sauce

No Mexican table is complete without a hot sauce of some kind. This one is excellent to have on hand when there's no time to make the traditional Salsa Picante.

Almost fill a small-necked, empty vinegar bottle with washed serrano chilies. (Serrano chilies are the smooth, green 1-1½-inch fresh chilies found in most Western markets.) Leave the chilies whole and fill the bottle with cider vinegar. Let the sauce stand for a week or so and then taste the vinegar for strength – it should be strong and nippy. As the serrano sauce is used, refill the bottle with vinegar. The chilies don't need to be changed for at least a year, maybe longer; just add more vinegar.

This can be used on frijoles (beans), rice, eggs, in fact on any food needing a dash of strength.

SALSA PICANTE

No meal is complete without Salsa Picante. Mention this sauce in any part of Mexico and everyone will know what you mean. It will keep in the refrigerator indefinitely or can be frozen. Mexicans make the sauce fresh every day.

½ cup chopped onions
1 cup chopped tomatoes or tomatillos
½ cup chopped Annaheim chilies or bell pepper
1-3 jalapeños, finely chopped
2 tablespoons cider vinegar
Pinch of sea salt
2 tablespoons vegetable oil
1 teaspoon raw cane sugar
1 teaspoon chopped fresh cilantro

Combine all the ingredients in a jar and refrigerate.

PICKLED JALAPEÑOS
Jalapeños en Escabache

1 8-ounce jar jalapeños or 1 cup chopped fresh jalapeños
1 15-ounce jar small onions
4 cups sliced carrots, cooked
4 tablespoons vegetable oil
2 tablespoons raw cane sugar
Pinch each of oregano, marjoram and thyme
4 cloves
2 cloves garlic
Tarragon vinegar to cover

Pack all the ingredients into jars and refrigerate. (This can be served at once or left to stand for a couple of days.)

Note: This same sauce can be made of fresh vegetables. Prepare the vegetables and add the remaining ingredients. Bring to the boil for 1 minute, then pack into jars and refrigerate.

CHILI RELLENO SAUCE
Salsa de Chilis Rellenos

1 cup tomato sauce
1 cup mushroom soup, diluted
1 teaspoon chili powder
¼ cup each of chopped onions and Ortega chilies
1 jalapeño chili, chopped
1 teaspoon each of oregano, garlic powder, celery seed,
   thyme, marjoram and cumin seed
½ teaspoon each of sea salt, chopped red pepper,
   mustard and ginger

Combine all the ingredients in a saucepan and simmer for 15 minutes. Serve this sauce over Chilis Rellenos (page 79) with tortillas, Salsa Picante, sour cream and grated cheese.

PIQUANT SWEET VEGETABLE RELISH
Salsa Picante y Dulce de los Legumbres

2 cups finely chopped chayotes
1 quart finely chopped cabbage
1 quart chopped tomatillos
3 fresh, green chilies, chopped
4 large onions, chopped
1 quart cider vinegar (or enough to cover)
6 of each – jalapeños, serrano chilies (whole and with stems)
4 cups raw cane sugar
1 teaspoon each of allspice, turmeric, mustard seed, garlic powder, celery seed, horseradish, cloves and chili powder
1 tablespoon each of sea salt, paprika and red hot chili seeds

1. Prepare all the ingredients and combine them in a large kettle.

2. Simmer for 1 hour, stirring frequently and then pack the sauce in hot sterilized jars and seal. Store for 3 weeks before serving.

SOUR CREAM COCKTAIL SAUCE FOR RAW VEGETABLES
Salsa de Coctel de Crema Agria para Legumbres Crudos

1 cup sour cream
1 teaspoon cider vinegar
¼ cup each of chopped pimento and black olives
¼ teaspoon each of sea salt, thyme, paprika and dill seed
Vegetable sticks and salted almonds, chopped or slivered

1. Combine the sour cream, vinegar and seasonings, then fold in the pimento and black olives.

2. Refrigerate until ready to use and serve with bowls of vegetable sticks. After dipping in the sauce, dip each stick into the almonds.

5. Tacos and Enchiladas

Those vegetarians who like soybean products can make tacos and enchiladas which appear as the real thing.

A taco is a warmed tortilla wrapped around refried beans, cheese and/or other fillings and seasoned with chilies, herbs and spices. This recipe is one of the easiest to make and it is a gourmet's delight.

For each taco you'll need approximately 2-3 tablespoons of textured vegetable protein "beef" or "pork" cut into tiny shreds. A very thin, warmed 4-5-inch flour tortilla is placed on a warmed plate. The cooked "meat" is placed across the tortilla just below the center line. A sprinkling of fresh, chopped coriander (cilantro), approximately 1 tablespoon of chopped onion and a teaspoon of liquid hot sauce is then added to the "meat". Roll the taco up tightly, salt it lightly and eat immediately.

An enchilada is also a tortilla wrapped around a filling, but in a different way.

Half fill a frying pan with vegetable oil and another with hot enchilada sauce (page 66). Dip the tortilla in the hot oil for 30 seconds, then in the hot sauce for another 30 seconds. Lay the tortilla on a warmed plate and fill it with your choice of filling, then roll it up. Make as many enchiladas as you want to serve and place two or three side by side on a warmed plate. Cover with the sauce in which the tortilla was dipped and spoon some grated cheese and sour cream over the top. Serve with bowls of goodies such as chopped onions, chopped fresh coriander, chopped Mexican green tomatoes or red tomatoes, chopped black olives, serrano sauce (page 59), lemon wedges, shredded lettuce or cabbage, grated cheese, whole jalapeños or serrano chilies, strips of pimento.

ENCHILADA SAUCE

½ cup of chopped onion and green pepper
2-3 cloves garlic, crushed or chopped
2 tablespoons each of whole wheat flour, chopped parsley and paprika
¼ teaspoon each of sea salt, freshly ground black pepper, clove, cinnamon, oregano, crushed cumin seed, marjoram, mustard, sage, celery seed and grated lemon rind
1 cup each of tomato sauce and V-8 or water
2 tablespoons cider vinegar
1-2 jalapeño chilies, chopped (fresh or canned)

1. Sauté the onion, green pepper, garlic, flour, parsley and paprika in the oil.

2. Add the seasonings and simmer the mixture for 3-4 minutes.

3. Stir in the tomato sauce, water, vinegar and chilies and simmer for 10 minutes or until the sauce has thickened and the aroma is delicious and tempting.

SOUR CREAM SAUCE
Salsa de Crema Agria

2 cups sour cream
¼ cup chopped black olives
1 tablespoon chopped pimento
2-3 dashes of a hot sauce

1. Combine the ingredients and spread the mixture over the enchiladas. Serve sprinkled with toasted sesame seeds.

To Toast Sesame Seeds
Spread sesame seeds on the bottom of a frying pan. Turn the heat to medium low and stir the seeds with a wooden spoon. Alternatively, shake the pan to prevent burning the seeds.

EGG OMELETTE AND CHILI
Enchilada de Huevo Espanol y Chili

1 omelette (see opposite)
3-4 strips Ortega chili
1 thin slice cheese
1 teaspoon salsa picante (page 60)

1. Place all the ingredients on a prepared tortilla (page 65), roll it up and place it on a warm serving dish. (Keep it warm and make as many enchiladas as are needed.)

2. Cover the tortilla with enchilada sauce (page 66) and sprinkle a generous portion of grated cheese over the top. Serve with enchilada accompaniments (page 65).

Omelette

1 egg
1 tablespoon water
¼ teaspoon paprika
1 tablespoon chopped onion
Dash of sea salt and freshly ground black pepper

1. Combine all the ingredients and fry on both sides in a teflon fry pan.

2. Lay the omelette on a prepared tortilla. (It is better to do one egg at a time so that the omelette will be flat.)

ENCHILADA WITH REFRIED BEANS AND CHILI
Enchilada de Frijoles Mexicanos y Chili

3 tablespoons refried beans (see opposite)
2½-3½ tablespoons grated cheese
3 strips Ortega chili
1 tablespoon each of chopped onion and coriander
1 teaspoon salsa picante (page 60) – optional

1. Spread the ingredients on one half of the prepared tortilla (page 65).

2. Roll it up and place it on a warm serving dish. (Keep it warm and make as many enchiladas as are needed.)

3. Cover the tortilla with enchilada sauce (page 66) and sprinkle with a generous portion of grated cheese and any of the enchilada accompaniments (page 65).

REFRIED BEANS AND CHILI
Frijoles Mexicanos

1 cup cooked beans, with juice
2 tablespoons vegetable oil
¼ cup each of tomato sauce and chopped onions
¼ teaspoon each of oregano, sea salt, freshly ground
    black pepper and crushed cumin seed
1 teaspoon chopped jalapeño chili

1. Mash the beans with the oil and sauté them until very
   dry.

2. Add the remaining ingredients and sauté the mixture
   again until very dry.

ENCHILADA WITH CHEESE AND CHILI
Enchilada de Queso y Chili

1 thin slice cheese
Cheese strips to spread across the tortilla
3-4 strips Ortega chili
1 tablespoon each of chopped onion and cilantro
1 teaspoon salsa picante (page 60) – optional

1. Spread the ingredients on one half of each prepared tortilla (page 65).

2. Roll up the tortilla and place it on a warm serving dish. (Keep it warm and make as many enchiladas as are needed.)

3. Cover the enchilada with a sour cream sauce (page 67) and sprinkle with a generous portion of toasted sesame seeds and any of the enchilada accompaniments (page 65).

ENCHILADA WITH VEGETABLES AND CHILIES
Enchilada de Legumbres y Chilis

Approx. 3 tablespoons cooked vegetables (see below)
1 tablespoon grated Parmesan cheese
3-4 strips Ortega chili
1 tablespoon each of chopped onion and cilantro
1 teaspoon salsa picante (page 60) – optional

1. Spread the ingredients on one half of the prepared tortilla (page 65).

2. Roll it up and place it on a warm serving dish. (Keep it warm and make as many enchiladas as are needed.)

3. Cover the tortilla with sour cream sauce (page 67) and sprinkle with a generous portion of grated cheese and any other enchilada accompaniments.

Cooked Vegetable Suggestions

Asparagus	Mushrooms
Broccoli	Onion
Cabbage	Potato
Carrots (grated)	Spinach
Cauliflower	Tomato
Eggplant	

ENCHILADA WITH TVP "MEAT"
Enchilada de Chili con "Carne"

This chili con carne can be prepared with tofu or any of the soybean-based "meats".

3 tablespoons cooked textured vegetable protein "meat"
1 tablespoon grated sharp cheese
1 teaspoon salsa picante (page 60)
1 tablespoon chopped mushrooms

1. Spread the ingredients on one half of a prepared tortilla (page 65).

2. Roll it up and place it on a warm serving dish. (Keep it warm and make as many enchiladas as are needed.)

3. Cover the tortilla with enchilada sauce (page 66) and sprinkle with a generous portion of grated cheese and any other enchilada accompaniments.

Note: Raisins and nuts are delicious with any soy "meat" recipes.

BLACK BEANS AND CHILIES
Enchilada de Frijoles Negros y Chili

3 tablespoons black beans, cooked and mashed
1 tablespoon grated Parmesan cheese
3-4 strips Ortega chili
1 tablespoon each of chopped onion and cilantro
1 teaspoon salsa picante (page 60) – optional

1. Spread the ingredients on one half of a prepared tortilla (page 65).

2. Roll it up and place it on a warm serving dish. (Keep it warm and make as many enchiladas as are needed.)

3. Cover the tortilla with sour cream sauce (page 67) and sprinkle with a generous portion of grated cheese and any other enchilada accompaniments.

FRUIT ENCHILADA
Enchilada de Fruta

3-4 tablespoons chopped fruit
1 tablespoons each of chopped nuts, raisins, maraschino cherries and candied ginger
Toasted coconut

1. Spread the ingredients over one half of the warm tortilla.

2. Roll it up and place it on a warm serving dish. (Keep it warm and make as many enchiladas as are needed.)

3. Cover the tortilla with sour cream sauce (page 67) and sprinkle with toasted coconut.

6. Main Meals

RICE AND MUSHROOM CASSEROLE
Cazuela de Arroz y Champinones

(Serves 6)

5 cups cooked brown rice
1½ pounds button mushrooms (stems removed)
1 cup each of grated cheese and fresh whole wheat
　breadcrumbs
½ cup each of chopped onions and melted butter
1 tablespoon chopped parsley
½ teaspoon each of sea salt, ginger, celery seed, freshly
　ground black pepper and chili powder
Chopped nuts

1. Place the rice and mushrooms in a casserole.

2. Combine the chopped mushroom stems, cheese, bread-crumbs, onions, butter, parsley and seasonings and spread the mixture over the rice and mushrooms.

3. Broil until the cheese is bubbly and garnish with nuts.

CHILI CON "CARNE"

(Serves 8)

2 pounds tofu
¼ cup vegetable oil
1 Ortega chili, chopped
1 tablespoon each of chili powder, cumin seed, oregano, paprika, raw cane sugar, chopped cilantro and chopped jalapeño chili
1 cup chopped onions
¼ cup *masa harina** moistened with ¼ cup water
2 cups mushroom or celery soup
2 cups tomato sauce
4 cups pinto beans, cooked

1. Cut the tofu into ½-inch cubes and sauté in oil.

2. Add chili, seasonings and onions, and fry until the onions become translucent.

3. Add the remaining ingredients and simmer for 30 minutes, stirring occasionally.

4. Serve with sourdough rolls or warmed tortillas, bowls of shredded cabbage, grated cheese, black olives, chopped tomatoes and salsa picante (page 60).

*Available in specialty food stores. Alternatively, use whole wheat flour.

STUFFED CHILIES
Chilis Rellenos

(Serves 6)

12 Ortega chilies (whole)
2 pounds cheese (Mexican if possible) cut into 12
  wedges
*Masa harina**
6 egg whites
6 egg yolks
½ teaspoon each of sea salt, red pepper flakes, garlic
  powder, paprika, chili powder, oregano, marjoram,
  tarragon and cumin seed

1. Fill the 12 chilies with the cheese wedges, being careful
   not to split the chilies. (If they should split, fasten them
   with a tooth.)

2. Moisten the outsides of the chilies and dip them into
   the flour. (If they are not coated with flour the beaten
   eggs won't stick.)

3. Whip the egg whites until stiff and beat the egg yolks
   until fluffy. Combine the whites, yolks and seasonings,
   by gently folding them together.

4. Dip the chilies into the egg mixture, one at a time, and
   place them in a frying pan of hot oil at 375°F. Fry on
   both sides until golden brown and then drain them for a
   minute or two on paper towels. Serve the chilies hot
   with salsa picante and chili relleno sauce (pages 60 and
   62), olives, refried beans and brown rice.

*Available at specialty food stores. See Useful Addresses
 (page 125).

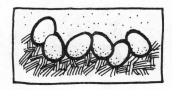

MACARONI AND CHEESE
Pasta y Queso

(Serves 6-8)

2 cups whole wheat macaroni or homemade whole
    wheat pasta (see page 81)
3 tablespoons butter
1 large onion, chopped
2 cloves garlic, minced
¼ cup whole wheat flour
2 cups milk
¾ teaspoon each of cumin seed, oregano and celery
    seed
1 7-ounce can green chilies, chopped
1 7-ounce can black olives, slivered
3 cups grated sharp cheese

1. Cook the macaroni in water according to the manu-
   facturer's directions and then drain.

2. Melt the butter in the frying pan, add the onion and
   garlic and cook until soft.

3. Stir in the flour and cook until bubbly.

4. Gradually stir in the milk to make a smooth and thick
   sauce.

5. Remove the pan from the heat and add the seasonings,
   chilies, olives and drained pasta. Stir until the pasta is
   well coated.

6. Layer the cheese and pasta in a buttered 3-quart
   casserole and bake, uncovered, at 400°F for 20 minutes
   or until the cheese is bubbly and the top is golden
   brown.

HOMEMADE PASTA

Homemade pasta is much tastier than the shop-bought kind. Try the following recipe to make your own:

4 eggs, beaten
½ cup milk
½ cup grated Parmesan cheese
3 cups sifted whole wheat flour

1. Combine the eggs and milk and add the Parmesan cheese and enough of the flour to make a stiff dough. (Add more flour if necessary.) Cover the dough and set it aside for 15 minutes.

2. Divide the dough in half and roll out each half very thinly on a floured surface.

3. Set the dough aside again for 20 minutes and roll each piece up loosely. Slice the rolls ¼ inch thick.

4. Unroll and spread out the pasta and leave it to dry for 2 hours.

5. Drop the pasta into boiling salted water and cook for approximately 10 minutes until easy to cut but not soft, then drain.

CHILI PASTA

(Serves 6)

1 pound whole wheat pasta (see page 81)
1 cup cream
¼ cup grated sharp cheese
¼ cup butter
2 cloves garlic
½ teaspoon each of onion powder, celery seed, allspice,
    sea salt and red pepper flakes
1⅓ cups tofu, drained and cut into 1-inch cubes
¼ cup vegetable oil
1 carton frozen peas
8 ounces button mushrooms
½ cup chopped Ortega chilies

1. Boil the pasta in salted water and while it is cooking, place a round dish or serving plate over the top of the pan.

2. Put the cream, cheese and butter into the serving dish. (This is to heat the serving plate and melt the butter.)

3. Sauté the garlic, seasonings and tofu in the oil and as soon as the tofu is browned, add the peas, mushrooms and chilies.

4. Remove the dish and drain the pasta when cooked. Combine all the ingredients and mix them together. Serve while still hot.

RICE BOATS
Chalupas de Arroz

(Serves 6)

3 cups cooked brown rice
2 tablespoons grated orange rind
3 tablespoons curry powder
½ teaspoon each of sea salt, freshly ground black
    pepper, ginger, nutmeg, chopped parsley and aniseed
1 cup mushrooms, slivered
½ cup walnuts
¼ cup sour cream
3 avocados
Raisins and candied ginger

1. Combine all the ingredients (except the avocados, raisins and candied ginger) while the rice is still hot.

2. Cut the avocados in half and remove the pit and skin. (Be careful not to break the halved avocados.)

3. Divide the rice among the avocados, filling the hollows and let the excess rice nestle around the avocadoes. Garnish with raisins and ginger.

Note: A cheese sauce could be served with this dish.

ONION PIE
Pay de Cebolla

(Serves 6)

4 cups cottage cheese, drained
1 teaspoon grated nutmeg
Whole wheat pastry for a 9-inch pie shell
1 cup chopped pimento
6 cups chopped onions
¼ cup each of sesame oil and chopped nuts
¼ teaspoon each of sea salt, freshly ground black
   pepper, dill seed, tarragon, basil, garlic powder and
   celery seed.
½ cup chopped Ortega chili
Sour cream, grated cheese and grated orange rind

1. Combine the cottage cheese and nutmeg and pat the mixture into the pie shell.

2. Spread the pimento on the cheese and pat it down.

3. Sauté the onion, oil, nuts, seasonings and chili and pat the mixture down on the pimento.

4. Bake the pie at 400°F for 20-30 minutes and garnish with sour cream, grated cheese and orange rind.

Note: This may be served hot or cold and can also be frozen and baked at a later date.

OMELETTE
Torta de Huevos

(Serves 1)

2 eggs, beaten
1 tablespoon each of water and vegetable oil
¼ cup grated cheese
1 tablespoon chopped Ortega chili
½ cup bean sprouts

1. Beat together the eggs and water until thick, then add the oil.

2. Pour the mixture into a buttered omelette pan, spread the cheese over the eggs, then add the chili and bean sprouts.

3. Bake at 350°F for 30 minutes or until golden brown.

Add any of the following, if desired:
¼ cup of chopped almonds
¼ cup of chopped black olives
¼ cup of chopped onions
¼ cup of chopped green tomatoes/tomatillos

SAUERKRAUT AND CHEESE CASSEROLE
Cazuela de Col Agria y Queso

(Serves 6)

1½ pounds sauerkraut, rinsed and drained
1 cup chopped onion
A little vegetable oil
3 tablespoons sesame seeds
2½ cups mashed potato
½ teaspoon each of sea salt, freshly ground black
   pepper and caraway seeds
2 teaspoons raw cane sugar
1 cup sour cream
1½ cups grated sharp cheese
Black olives and Ortega chili strips

1. Sauté the sauerkraut and onions in the oil, then add the
   seeds, potato, seasonings, sugar and sour cream.

2. Divide the mixture among six individual casseroles or
   place it in one large casserole.

3. Sprinkle with the cheese and grill until it bubbles.
   Garnish with the olives and chili.

STUFFED ONIONS CASSEROLE
Cazuela de Cebollas Rellenas

(Serves 6)

6 large onions
¾ cup melted butter
4 tablespoons chopped parsley
½ teaspoon each of mustard, sea salt, freshly ground
   black pepper, garlic powder, celery seed, paprika and
   chili powder
½ cup grated sharp cheese
1 jalapeño chili, chopped
6 mushrooms
6 large cabbage leaves, semi-cooked
3 cups lentils, cooked
1½ cups grated cheese
Paprika

1. Peel the onions and simmer them for 15 minutes, then remove at least half of the centers to form cups.

2. Mix the chopped onion centers, butter, parsley, seasonings, cheese, chili and chopped mushroom stems.

3. Fill the onions with the mixture and block the ends of the onions with the mushroom caps, then encase each onion in a cabbage leaf. (First place the leaves into boiling water for a few minutes.)

4. Put the lentils into a buttered casserole and cover with the stuffed onions.

5. Sprinkle the grated cheese over the top and bake at 375°F for 30-45 minutes. Sprinkle with paprika.

VEGETABLE CASSEROLE
Cazuela de Legumbres

(Serves 6)

1 can mushroom soup, diluted
½ cup grated sharp cheese
1 jalapeño chili, chopped
¼ teaspoon each of sea salt, freshly ground black
    pepper, garlic powder, onion powder, celery seed
    and ginger
6 cups leftover vegetables
¼ cups chopped pimento
1 cup chopped nuts

1. Combine the soup, cheese, chili and seasonings and
   pour the mixture over any combination of vegetables
   in a large casserole.

2. Bake at 350°F for 30-45 minutes. Garnish with pimento
   and nuts.

SPINACH CHEESELETTES
Cazuela de Espinaca

(Serves 6)

3 cups bean sprouts
3 cups cooked spinach
5 cups grated cheese
1 each – tomato, onion, jalapeño chili, Ortega chili (all
   chopped)
¼ teaspoon each of sea salt, cilantro, mustard, red chili
   seeds and ginger
Sour cream, sliced apples and chopped walnuts

1. Combine all of the above ingredients (except the sour
   cream, apples and walnuts) gently.

2. Spread the mixture in six individual buttered casseroles
   or one large casserole and broil until the cheese is
   bubbly. Garnish with the sour cream, apples and nuts.

STUFFED ZUCCHINI WITH LENTILS
Calabacitas Rellenas con Lentejas Asada

(Serves 6)

5 cups lentils, cooked
3 pounds zucchini, halved and scraped out
¾ cup chopped onion
¼ cup sesame oil
3 cups fresh whole wheat breadcrumbs
1½ cups grated sharp cheese
½ teaspoon each of sea salt, freshly ground black
    pepper, chili powder, horseradish, allspice and garlic
    powder
Sour cream and slivered mushrooms

1. Divide the lentils among six individual buttered
   casseroles or use one large buttered casserole.

2. Place the zucchini on the lentils, then gently combine
   the onions, oil, breadcrumbs, cheese and seasonings.

3. Pile the mixture into the zucchini and broil until the
   cheese bubbles. Garnish with sour cream and
   mushrooms.

TINY ONIONS IN SOUR CREAM ON RICE
Cebollitas en Crema Agria con Arroz

(Serves 6)

1½ cups brown rice
1½ pounds tiny onions, peeled
¼ cup sesame oil
1 cup sour cream
¼ teaspoon each of mace, nutmeg, sea salt, red pepper,
    mustard, paprika, horseradish, celery seed and garlic
    powder
Orange slices and slivered almonds

1. Cook the rice until tender and place it in a buttered
   casserole.

2. Peel the onions and sauté them in the oil.

3. Stir the sour cream and seasonings into the onions, and
   pour the mixture over the rice.

4. Place the casserole in the oven at 350°F for approximately 15 minutes. Garnish with the orange slices and
   almonds.

CURRIED RICE CASSEROLE
Cazuela de Arroz con Curri

(Serves 6)

1 can mushroom soup, undiluted
1 cup coconut milk
3-6 tablespoons curry powder
1 tablespoon lemon juice
¼ teaspoon grated orange rind
1 tablespoon slivered candied ginger
¼ teaspoon each of sea salt, mustard and mace
1½ cups brown rice
Orange slices, parsley and nuts

1. Whisk together the soup, coconut milk, curry powder, lemon juice and orange rind.

2. Add the candied ginger and seasonings and heat the mixture but don't allow it to boil.

3. Cook the rice until tender and place it in a buttered casserole.

4. Pour the soup mixture over the rice and bake at 350°F for approximately 15 minutes. Garnish with the orange slices, parsley and nuts.

CLIVE BIRCH

RICE, LENTILS AND CABBAGE CASSEROLE
Cazuela de Arroz, Lentejas y Col

(Serves 8-10)

3 cups lentils, cooked
3 cups cooked brown rice
3 cups grated cheese
2 cups tomato sauce
1 cup water
⅓ cup each of chopped onion, chopped pimento and
   Ortega chili
¼ teaspoon each of sea salt, cayenne, mustard, allspice,
   tarragon, thyme, oregano and marjoram
2 heads of cabbage, leaves separated
Sour cream and black olives

1. Place the lentils, rice and cheese in 3 separate bowls and make a mixture of the tomato sauce, water, onion, pimento, chili and seasonings, then add one-third of the tomato mixture to each of the three dishes.

2. Cover the bottom and sides of a large casserole or baking dish with the cabbage leaves and cover the cabbage leaves with a little of the lentil mixture.

3. Cover the lentils with more cabbage leaves and cover these with a little of the rice mixture. Cover the rice with more cabbage leaves and cover these with a little of the cheese mixture.

4. Continue layering the ingredients until the casserole is full, with cabbage leaves on top. Pack the mixture down fairly lightly by pushing with the heel of the hand.

5. Bake at 350°F for 45 minutes to 1 hour and garnish with sour cream and black olives.

Note: This dish can be served hot or cold; it can also be frozen and baked later.

BROILED TOMATOES WITH LENTILS
Jitomates con Lentejas Asados

(Serves 6)

3 cups lentils, cooked
1 cup each of slivered mushrooms and whole wheat
    breadcrumbs
½ cup chopped onions
4 tablespoons slivered ripe olives
¼ teaspoon each of sea salt, freshly ground black
    pepper, mustard, cloves, dill seed and garlic powder
6 tomatoes, halved
3 cups grated cheese
Sour cream and grated orange rind

1. Spread the lentils on the bottom of a large casserole.

2. Combine the mushrooms, breadcrumbs, onions, olives
   and seasonings and spread the mixture over the lentils.

3. Lay the tomatoes cut-side down on top and spread the
   cheese over them, then broil until the cheese bubbles.
   Garnish with sour cream and orange rind.

EGGPLANT AND ZUCCHINI CASSEROLE
Cazuela de Berenjena y Calabacita

(Serves 6)

1½ cups chopped tomatoes
½ cup each of chopped onion and chopped Ortega chili
4 cups grated cheese
1 cup whole wheat breadcrumbs
¼ teaspoon each of sea salt, freshly ground black
   pepper, ground ginger, coriander and cumin
1 tablespoon chopped parsley
2½ cups cooked eggplant
1½ cups cooked zucchini
Sour cream and grated carrots

1. Combine the tomatoes, onion, chili, cheese, breadcrumbs, oil, seasonings and parsley.

2. Layer the eggplants and zucchini in a buttered casserole
   with the tomato mixture.

3. Bake at 350°F for 20 minutes or until the cheese is
   bubbly. Garnish with sour cream and grated carrots.

BEET CASSEROLE WITH CHEESE
Cazuela de Betabeles con Queso

(Serves 6)

4 cups cooked, thinly sliced beets
1 cup grated cheese
1 cup sour cream
1½ cups whole wheat breadcrumbs
¼ cup sesame oil
1 tablespoon chopped parsley
¼ teaspoon each of sea salt, freshly ground black
    pepper, ginger, thyme, oregano, garlic powder and
    celery seed
Raisins and maraschino cherries

1. Combine all the ingredients (except the raisins and
   cherries) and put the mixture into a buttered casserole.

2. Bake at 350°F for 30-40 minutes or until the cheese is
   bubbly. Garnish with the raisins and cherries.

WHIPPED CARROTS IN SOUR CREAM
Zanahorias Batidas con Crema Agria

(Serves 6)

5 cups carrots, cooked
¼ cup each of raw cane sugar, sour cream and chopped
   Ortega chili
¼ teaspoon each of ground cloves, horseradish, sea salt,
   cayenne pepper, celery seed, rosemary and thyme
Sour cream
1 cup chopped walnuts
Grated coconut and grated carrot

1. Combine the carrots, sugar, sour cream, chili and
   seasoning in a blender.

2. Put the mixture in a casserole and broil it until bubbly
   and heated through. Garnish with sour cream, walnuts,
   coconut and raw carrot.

CHEESE AND CHILI CASSEROLE
Chilaquiles de Queso y Chilis

(Serves 8)

8 tortillas (see page 22)
1 cup chopped Ortega chilies
2 cups chopped tomatoes
2 cups chopped onions
¼ teaspoon each of cilantro, sea salt, freshly ground
    black pepper, chili powder, thyme and rosemary
2 cups grated sharp cheese

1. Divide the tortillas among eight individual casseroles or use one large baking dish.

2. Spread the chilies, tomatoes, onions and seasonings over the tortillas and sprinkle the cheese over the top.

3. Bake at 375°F for 30 minutes or until the cheese bubbles.

STUFFED CHILI CASSEROLE
(Serves 4-6)

3-4 tortillas (see page 22)
1 7-ounce can Ortega chilies
½ cup chopped onions
1 cup grated sharp cheese
4 eggs
5 tablespoons water
½ teaspoon baking powder
¼ cup grated Parmesan cheese
Chopped cilantro or parsley

1. Layer the tortillas on the bottom and sides of a 1½-quart buttered casserole.

2. Add the chilies (split open) and the onions and cheese.

3. Beat the eggs thoroughly and mix in the water, baking powder and flour.

4. Pour the egg mixture over the chilies and cheese and sprinkle with Parmesan cheese.

5. Bake, uncovered, at 375°F for 30 minutes or until golden brown. Sprinkle with cilantro or parsley.

Note: Serve this dish with brown rice, chopped onion, chopped tomatoes and shredded cabbage.

*Available at specialty food stores. See Useful Addresses (page 125).

7. Soybeans

Soybeans are full of vitamins A, E, K, B_1, B_2, potassium and lecithin. They are manufactured in many forms: grits, meal, powder, flour, nuts, tofu, pastas and also made-up to resemble different types of meat (Tvp).

To Cook Soybeans

½ pound (1 cup) dry soybeans
4 cups water
4 tablespoons vegetable oil
1 tablespoon sea salt

1. Combine the beans and water and boil them for 3 minutes.

2. Set the beans aside to soak for 12 hours, then add the oil and salt and simmer for 2-3 hours.

SOYBEAN PATTIES
Empanadas de Frijoles Soyas

(Serves 6)

2 cups soybeans, cooked and mashed
1 cup cooked brown rice
¼ cup chopped Ortega chilies
2 eggs
1 tablespoon cider vinegar
1 cup apple sauce
2 tablespoons chopped onion
½ teaspoon each of sea salt, red pepper flakes, garlic
    powder, celery seed and oregano
2-3 cardamom seeds
2 cups whole wheat breadcrumbs
Lemon slices, chopped onions, salsa picante and
    pimento

1. In a blender, purée the soybeans, rice, chilies, eggs,
   vinegar and apple sauce.

2. Put the mixture into a bowl and add the onions and
   seasonings.

3. Shape the mixture into small patties and roll them in
   breadcrumbs.

4. Bake at 375°F for 45 minutes and garnish with lemon
   slices. Serve with bowls of onions and salsa picante and
   strips of pimento.

DRY-ROASTED SOYBEANS
Frijoles Soyas Asadas

Sprinkle a generous amount of sea salt on a baking sheet and spread cooked soybeans, strained and towel-dried, over the salt. Sprinkle more sea salt over the beans and roast them, uncovered, at 350°F for 45 minutes or until browned and crisp to the bite. Leave to cool and store the beans in an airtight container.

Note: If the beans become soft and moist, dry them out on a baking sheet in the oven at a very low heat.

FRIED SOYBEANS
Frijoles Soyas Fritas

(Serves 4)

2 cups soybeans, cooked
2 tablespoons sesame oil
½ cup each of chopped onion, green pepper and tomato
½ teaspoon each of sea salt, garlic and onion powder, celery seed, cloves, oregano, mustard and chili powder
½ jalapeño, chopped

1. Combine and sauté all the ingredients for 15-20 minutes or until golden brown. Serve hot with whole wheat sourdough bread or rolls.

SOYBEAN CASSEROLE
Cazuela de Frijoles Soyas

(Serves 8)

2½ cups soybeans, cooked
2½ cups each of apple juice and tomatoes, skinned and
    crushed
1 tablespoon each of chili powder and cider vinegar
6 cloves garlic, minced
1-2 stale tortillas, crushed
3 jalapeño chilies, chopped
½ teaspoon each of cloves, oregano, red pepper flakes,
    mustard, tarragon and fenugreek
2 teaspoons sea salt
2 cups grated strong cheese
½ cup wheat germ
Sour cream, chopped cilantro and chopped walnuts

1. Combine the soybeans with all the ingredients, except
   the cheese and wheat germ, cream, cilantro and walnuts.

2. Divide the mixture among eight buttered, individual
   casseroles or use one large casserole and sprinkle the
   cheese and wheat germ over the top.

3. Broil until golden brown or until the cheese is bubbly.
   Garnish with sour cream, cilantro and chopped walnuts.

8. Vegetable Side-dishes

WINTER SQUASH
Calabaza

Choose a calabaza or other winter squash. The harder the shell, the better. Cut the squash into 2-inch squares and remove the seeds and membrane. Place the pieces in a frying pan with the shell side down. Mix and add the following to the squash:

½ cup raw cane sugar
¼ teaspoon sea salt
½ teaspoon aniseed
1 cup water

1. Cover the pan and simmer the mixture for 1 hour or until the squash is cooked.

2. Remove the lid and baste the squash until almost all of the liquid is absorbed. Serve hot or cold.

SAUTÉED CHESTNUTS
Costanas Fritas

(Serves 4-6)

2 pounds chestnuts, shelled
½ cup each of butter and chopped nuts
¼ teaspoon each of sea salt, celery seed, poppy seed and
  paprika

1. Shell and boil the chestnuts in water to cover for about
   20 minutes, then drain them.

2. Sauté the chestnuts in the butter, nuts and seasonings
   and serve hot and golden brown.

CHESTNUTS AND MUSHROOMS
Costañas y Champiñones

(Serves 4-6)

1 pound chestnuts, shelled
1 pound tiny button mushrooms, whole
¼ cup peanut oil or butter
2 tablespoons whole wheat flour
1½ cups sour cream
¼ teaspoon each of sea salt, paprika and grated lemon
  rind
Black olives, grated mild cheese and parsley

1. Boil the chestnuts in water to cover for 20 minutes, then drain them and cut the chestnuts into quarters.

2. Sauté the chestnuts and mushrooms in the oil or butter.

3. Add the flour and stir it in to thicken the mixture.

4. Add the sour cream and seasonings and simmer the mixture until it bubbles. Garnish with olives, cheese and parsley.

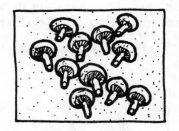

FRIED EGGPLANT
Berenjena Fritada

(Serves 6-8)

1 small eggplant
2-3 eggs
*Masa harina**
Chili powder
Ortega chilies (1½ for each slice of eggplant)
Vegetable oil for deep-frying
1 cup grated sharp cheese
Sour cream and paprika

1. Skin and slice the eggplant into 1-inch rounds, then soak them in salted water for 1 hour.

2. Drain and dip each slice into the flour and sprinkle with chili powder.

3. Split the chilies in half lengthways and dip each half into the flour.

4. Beat the eggs until stiff (beat the whites and yolks separately and then mix them gently.)

5. Dip the floured eggplant into the beaten eggs and then dip the chilies. As each piece is dipped into the eggs it should be placed in the hot vegetable oil (at 375°F and fried until golden brown. (It depends on the size of your deep-fryer as to how many of these you can cook at a time. Don't set the vegetables down after dipping in the egg; they must be cooked at once after dipping.)

*Available at specialty food stores. See Useful Addresses (page 125).

CORN ON THE COB
Elote

Cook corn on the cob in the usual way and then roll the hot corn in the following:

1 dish of melted butter with garlic and chili powder
1 dish of sour cream
1 dish of grated Parmesan cheese

Eat while hot and dripping. Several napkins will be needed for this. Even though this is a messy dish, it is well worth the trouble of the cleaning up process afterwards!

9. Desserts

CHOCOLATE CAKE
Pastel de Chocolate

(Serves 8-12)

2 cups whole wheat flour
1 cup raw cane sugar
½ cup cocoa or carob powder
2 teaspoons baking soda
½ teaspoon sea salt
1 teaspoon cinnamon
1 cup chopped almonds
1 cup each of water and mayonnaise
1 teaspoon pure vanilla extract

1. Sift together the flour, sugar, cocoa or carob, soda, salt and cinnamon.

2. Add the nuts and mix them in with the wet ingredients.

3. Bake at 350°F for 35 minutes or until cooked through.

For Icing:
Mix finely ground raw cane sugar with almond extract, a dash of cinnamon and enough water to make a runny icing. Pour this over the cake while still warm (not hot).

ALMOND TORTE
Torte de Almendras

(Serves 12-18)

2½ cups whole wheat flour
½ cup ground almonds, toasted
⅓ cup raw cane sugar
¼ teaspoon sea salt
¾ cup butter
⅓ cup cold water

1. Combine all the ingredients and divide the dough into thirds.

2. Roll each part into equal rounds, 8 inches in diameter. (Use an 8-inch pie plate to cut around and lay the rounds on ungreased baking sheets.)

3. Bake at 375°F for 10-12 minutes or until light brown.

For Filling:
4 cups chopped fruit (mango, papaya or other Mexican fruit)
1 cup crushed pineapple (in its own juice)
2 cups heavy cream, whipped
1 teaspoon pure almond extract
2 cups almonds, toasted and chopped

1. Combine the ingredients and spread the mixture evenly on the three bases, then stack one on top of the other.

2. Press down gently and chill the torte for 2-3 hours. Cut with a sharp knife.

Note: If you like, extra almonds may be used to decorate the sides of the torte.

BUÑUELOS

Fry some tortillas (page 22) in deep vegetable fat until crispy and light brown. Drain, but while still hot, cover with a mixture of raw cane sugar and cinnamon. Serve hot or cold. These are very delicate, so handle them with care. They absorb moisture quickly too, so it is better to make them only minutes before serving, unless you have a way to keep them free of moisture.

SWEET POTATO PUDDING
Cajeta de Comote con Pina

(Serves 4-6)

2 cups sweet potato, cooked and mashed
1 cup crushed pineapple (in its own juice)
1 cup raw cane sugar
1 teaspoon cinnamon
¼ teaspoon each of cloves, sea salt and mace
¾ cup ground almonds
Whipped cream and chopped almonds

1. Mix all the ingredients except the cream and chopped almonds, and simmer, stirring constantly over low heat until the mixture forms a mass and the bottom of the pan is visible. (The mixture will lose its gloss and all of the moisture will have been absorbed.)

2. Transfer the mixture to a serving dish, cover with whipped cream and sprinkle some nuts on top.

Note: This dish is delicious either hot or cold.

BREAD PUDDING
Capirotada

(Serves 6-8)

1 cup raw cane sugar
1 teaspoon cinnamon
2 cups boiling water
2 teaspoons butter
6 slices whole wheat toast
1 cup grated cheese
1 cup raisins
Whipped cream and chopped walnuts

1. Caramelize the sugar in a saucepan.

2. Add the cinnamon and hot water and stir until the sugar is dissolved.

3. Add the butter and layer the bread, cheese and raisins in a casserole.

4. Pour the syrup mixture over the top and bake the pudding at 350°F for 30 minutes or until most of the moisture has been absorbed. Serve hot or cold with whipped cream and nuts.

10. Drinks

PINEAPPLE PUNCH
Tepache

(Makes 16 8-ounce cups)

1 large fresh pineapple
1 stick cinnamon
8 cloves
3 quarts water
2 cups barley
8 cups raw cane sugar

1. Grind all of the pineapple (skin, peelings and fruit) and add the cinnamon, cloves and water.

2. Leave the mixture to stand for 2 days at room temperature in a large crock.

3. Boil the barley in 1 quart of water until the grain bursts. Leave it to cool and then mix in the pineapple mixture and the sugar.

4. Let the drink ferment for 1 to 2 days, then strain it through a sieve and serve over ice.

SANGRITA

(Makes 6 8-ounce cups)

This drink is a must if serving real Mexican foods. Whereas sangria means "blood of the widow", I have never known if "sangrita" means "a little blood" or "somewhat like blood", or the "little widow". Whichever term is used, it is a heartwarming drink and so piquant that a "wow" is the usual exclamation after just one sip. Have a cold bottle of beer handy or a sweet drink which will usually put out the "fire".

Sangria is sometimes made with tequila but sangrita is made without.

3 cups tomato juice
2 cups pure orange juice
1 cup pure lemon juice
1 teaspoon each of paprika, chili powder and coriander
  seed, crushed
¼ teaspoon each of sea salt, freshly ground black
  pepper, oregano, marjoram, cumin seed, crushed
  garlic powder, onion powder and celery seed, crushed
1-3 jalapeños, finely chopped

1. Combine all the ingredients in a 2-quart pitcher. Refrigerate for several hours and then serve in very small glasses – it is easier to let a guest ask for more than to scrape him off the ceiling if he has indulged himself indiscriminately in this hot spicy drink!

CIDER WITH CINNAMON
Sidra con Canela

(Makes 40 8-ounce cups)

2 cups pure lemon juice
1 teaspoon grated nutmeg
8 cloves
4 cinnamon sticks
1 ginger root (2 inches long)
1 tablespoon grated orange rind
2 cups raw cane sugar
4 quarts grape soda
2 quarts bitter-lemon soda
4 quarts apple cider
1 orange

1. Boil the first 7 ingredients for 5 minutes, then remove the saucepan from the heat and cool and chill the mixture.

2. Add the grape soda, bitter lemon and cider and pour the drink into a punch bowl.

3. Cut thin slices of orange into the punch and add flower blossoms if desired.

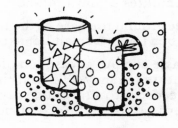

FLAMED COFFEE
Café Flambé

(Makes 20 demitasse cups)

1 lemon, thinly sliced
1 orange, thinly sliced
1 10-ounce bottle maraschino cherries, including liquid
10 cloves
1 stick cinnamon
1 teaspoon aniseed, crushed
¼ teaspoon cardamom seeds, crushed
1 cup apple cider
1 cup raw cane sugar
8 cups water
¾ cups powdered coffee
3½ tablespoons raw cane sugar
1 cup 90% proof brandy

1. Combine all the ingredients down to and including the 1 cup of sugar in a large punch bowl. Cover with a loose lid and set it aside in a warm place to ferment for 3-4 days, stirring occasionally. (If fermentation takes place before the time to use it, refrigerate it. If fermentation has not taken place by the time to serve it, don't worry – just use it as it is.)

2. Pull the fruit and spices to the center of the bowl.

3. Bring the water and powdered coffee to the boil and simmer for 5 minutes or until full-bodied.

4. Pour the coffee around the base of the fruit and spices and place the bowl over a small flame or gentle heat.

5. In each demitasse cup put a teaspoon of sugar and 1-2 teaspoons of heated brandy. (To heat the brandy, put the quantity needed into a tiny saucepan or soup ladle and heat it over a gas flame. Be careful not to ignite it.)

6. Pour 4 tablespoons of heated brandy over the fruits and spices in the bowl, taking care not to mix the brandy into the liquid or it won't ignite.

7. Ignite the brandy in the demitasse cups and serve the drink to guests while your partner is igniting the punch bowl.

8. Turn out the lights and try to serve the ignited *café flambé* while it is flaming.

YOGURT COOLER
Bulgar Frio

(Makes 3-4 servings)

2 cups natural yogurt or buttermilk
½ cup chopped cucumber
1 cup bitter lemon
¼ teaspoon each of chopped parsley, sea salt, grated
  orange peel and ginger
Ground cinnamon

1. Blend all the ingredients except the cinnamon.

2. Refrigerate the drink for at least 1 hour before serving
   in tall glasses, sprinkled with cinnamon.

Useful Addresses

Casa Moneo
210 West 14th Street
New York, N.Y. 10014

Mexican fresh, dried and canned ingredients, cooking
equipment; mail orders.

H. Roth and Son
1577 First Avenue
New York, N.Y. 10022

Index